The Time of
Jesus

Lois Rock

LION

To Steve

Bible references for the stories in this book

Notes on the crafts

Each item in this book is closely modelled on ones that historians and archaeologists know to have been in use at the time of Jesus. The materials suggested for making them have been chosen to give a realistic effect, but are nevertheless readily obtainable today from supermarkets, department stores and craft suppliers. The skills demanded are within reach of young people from the age of eight, but, as with all craftwork and cooking, adult encouragement and supervision will be needed to see the projects through safely.

When planning to undertake any of these projects, remember above all that, in the time of Jesus, people had to make the best of whatever they had to hand: to improvise, to reuse things that were old—in short, to cut their coat according to their cloth! Whenever you have to do the same, you are, in a different way, entering into the spirit of the times!

Introduction

Imagine growing up in the time of Jesus… being part of the world that he lived in… seeing the same sights… sharing the same meals… taking part in the same customs and traditions.

If you could really do that, you would discover that the story unfolds in a lively and bustling community in Palestine, in the time of the Roman empire. There are mothers with noisy babies taking care of the house and preparing meals for their household; fathers working at their trade or on the land; religious teachers worrying about how to lead people to see the difference between right and wrong… and little children playing in the sunshine, looking for something to brighten up the day, flocking to listen to the storytelling preacher with a lively northern accent, the one that people call Jesus.

This book is designed to help you recreate that world with twenty different craft and cooking activities: clothes and food, and familiar objects from home, school and synagogue. Each one is set alongside an episode from the life of Jesus, and the episodes build to provide a complete picture of his life and teaching.

Contents

1_ A baby is born

The arrival of a new baby turns family life upside down!

When Jesus was born, about 2,000 years ago, no one knew just how *much* his life was going to change not just his family but the whole world. Indeed, as the time for his birth drew closer, it was really only his mother, Mary, and other relatives who were interested.

Mary must have been busy getting ready the things she knew a baby needs. It was the custom in her day to wrap a newborn baby snugly in a blanket and then use long strips of cloth—swaddling bands—to hold baby and blanket in a neat little bundle. The baby felt safe and secure, and was easy for the mother to pick up and carry.

Swaddling bands were what every baby was wrapped in at the time of Jesus. Sometimes they were embroidered. Perhaps Jesus' mother spent time lovingly embroidering swaddling bands so as to have something special for her firstborn son.

Mary is having a baby!

Mary felt happy. Life was going just as it should. She had grown up a good daughter. Now her family had arranged for her to marry a man who would take care of her always: Joseph, the carpenter of Nazareth.

It was a time to dream happy dreams as she busied herself around the house. Then, one day, a sudden brightness made her look up.

'Oh!' Mary caught her breath. Someone was in the house. And not just an ordinary someone. This stranger, shining brightly in white and gold, was surely *an angel*.

The angel spoke: 'Peace be with you. The Lord God is with you, and has greatly blessed you. So don't be afraid. You will become pregnant and have a baby son. You will call him Jesus. He will be known as God's son. He will be God's special king.'

Moments later, when the angel had gone, Mary wondered why she had asked so few questions—why she had replied as she did: 'I will do what God wants.'

When she found that she was pregnant, she had to tell other people. Joseph was angry. The whisper went out that he was not going to marry Mary now.

Then, something made him change his mind. He promised to take care of her and her baby. He helped her as they prepared to become a family.

The flat roof of a little house like the one that Mary may have lived in.

Swaddling bands

You will need

- scissors
- cross-stitch fabric
- matching sewing thread
- coloured embroidery yarn
- cross-stitch needle
- graph paper and coloured pencils (to match your embroidery yarn)
- masking tape

What to do

1 Cut the fabric into strips about 30 mm wide. Follow a thread in the weave of the fabric as you cut. Join the strips together using matching thread and a strong back stitch. Swaddling bands need to be at least 2 m long to wrap round a baby-sized bundle!

2 Turn in a hem of about 5 mm all round, following a thread in the weave. Use coloured embroidery thread to stitch the hem in place with a simple in-and-out stitch.

3 Count the number of holes across the strip now. Then count out the same number of squares across the graph paper and work out your design. Take care not to make any stitches span more than three holes.

4 Thread the needle with about 45 cm of embroidery yarn at a time. Push the needle through from the wrong side. Leave a tail about 6 cm long and, using masking tape, tape it against the fabric on a part you are NOT going to stitch.

5 Stitch the design. When the yarn is almost used up, push the needle through to the wrong side and weave the tail of yarn through the back of the worked stitches. Take the tape off the starting length of yarn, rethread it and weave that through the back of the worked stitches close by. Continue with more thread.

★ Long bands will take a long time to stitch. Work a simple motif every 15 cm if you want a good effect more quickly.

★ You can do this project as part of a group. Each person works on an unhemmed strip. At the end, you join the strips together and hem them as a single piece.

A stone manger

You will need

- a cardboard box, large enough to hold a baby (or baby doll)

- a larger box, cut to the same height but about 10 cm wider and longer

- masking tape

- strips of paper, such as newsprint or copy paper

- a bowl of wallpaper paste, thinned so it is as runny as double cream

- large paintbrushes

- acrylic or emulsion paints in pale stone colours, such as grey and white

What to do

1 Centre the smaller box inside the larger one. Use strips of masking tape to hold the inner box central.

2 Roughly tear some of the box trimmings and tape these rough shapes on the outside box to help give the uneven look of hewn stone.

3 Dip the strips of paper in the wallpaper paste and lay them over the gap between the boxes, smoothing the extra paper down on either side. Use three or four layers for strength. Then dip more strips in the paste and cover the box, wrinkling and twisting the paper to give the box a rough finish.

4 Leave to dry for a couple of days.

5 Paint inside and outside with a single pale colour and leave to dry. Then stipple on a couple of darker colours by dabbing paint on with a lightly-filled brush, to give a stone effect.

2 A borrowed room

What would it be like to have a baby? Mary must have dreamed of how she would like everything to be perfect when the time came.

But the reality was not to be like that.

A layer of straw and a wool blanket helps turn a cold stone manger into a cosy bed for a baby. Even so, Mary must have wondered about the angel's message as she leaned over her baby. Was her son really God's king, born in such a humble shelter?

The baby in the manger

Months later, Mary and Joseph had to travel many miles south, to Bethlehem. The Romans who ruled their land had ordered everyone to go to their home town to register their names. There was no arguing with the order.

That's how they came to be far from home, just at the time when Mary was expecting her baby to be born. They jostled among strangers in the unfamiliar town.

'This is so frightening,' thought Mary. 'I'm sure the pains I feel are the baby coming.'

'I can't find anywhere to stay,' worried Joseph. 'It's getting desperate.'

'You'll not find a decent room in Bethlehem now,' said the person at the next place they enquired. 'Too many people are travelling for this census. But the lady needs to lie down, I can see. So let me show you a stable we could turn into a makeshift shelter for you.'

There, in the place that was no place to stay, Mary's first baby was born—the one that an angel had said was God's little baby king. Joseph had the clever idea of making a deep bed of straw in the stone manger where people usually put food for the farm animals. And Mary had brought with her the wrapping blanket and the specially embroidered swaddling bands.

According to an old tradition, the 'stable' in Bethlehem was a cave. The manger was probably made from a hollowed block of limestone.

3 Growing up in the Jewish faith

Joseph and Mary took good care of the little baby Jesus, keeping him from harm. Some time after his birth they returned to Nazareth. Here, he grew up to know the customs and traditions of his people.

One thing that Jesus most surely learned to read and write was the 'confession of faith' of the Jewish community, from the Hebrew scriptures. It is called the *shema*, which is the first word of the confession.

Hear, O Israel,

the Lord is our God,

the Lord alone.

The Hebrew letters go from right to left like this:

l'rsy 'ms

wnyhl' hwhy

dh' hwhy

Here are the same words with vowels, reading from left to right:

sh^ema' yisra'el

yahweh 'elohenu

yahweh 'echad

Jesus grows up

As Jesus grew into a boy, Joseph began to teach him his own trade: how to be a carpenter, working with wood and stone.

When Jesus was about seven he went to school at the synagogue with other boys. There, he learned to read the special books of his people—the Jewish scriptures, written in an old language called Hebrew. He learned the stories of his people's past, and how they had come to believe in a God who took special care of them.

Jesus listened hard. He asked questions so he could really understand.

When Jesus was twelve, he went with his family to the city of Jerusalem. Outside the towering temple where his people came to worship their God, the cleverest and most learned scholars of the faith met under the colonnade.

Jesus went up to them boldly.

His family knew nothing of this. They even began the long journey home with other pilgrims before they noticed he was not with the party. When, at last, they found him, they were astonished to see him asking questions and answering others with great wisdom. Mary wondered all the more: before he was born, an angel had said that her Jesus would be called God's son.

A carpenter's workshop from the time of Jesus.

◎ Wooden writing tablets. The recess holds a thin layer of soft wax. You can write in the wax with a pointed wooden stylus, smoothing over the wax to get rid of mistakes.
Perhaps Joseph helped Jesus make his own writing tablets to use at school.

A writing tablet

You will need

- short plank of balsa for the base
- thin strip of balsa for the frame
- craft knife, cutting mat and steel ruler
- sandpaper
- PVA glue
- sheet of beeswax
- old saucepan with a pouring lip
- pencil lengths of 5 mm dowel
- pencil-sharpener

★Ask a grown-up to advise and help when cutting wood.

What to do

1 Cut the base wood to size using a craft knife lined up against the steel ruler on the cutting mat. Sandpaper the edges smooth.

2 Cut two strips of wood to fit the long sides of the rectangle, and two shorter pieces to fit the space at the top and bottom. Sandpaper all the pieces smooth.

3 Spread glue on the underside of the strips and the border part of the main rectangle. Fit the strips carefully in place. Cover the tablet with a flat, heavy object such as a book and allow the glue to set.

4 Melt a sheet of beeswax over a gentle heat in the saucepan. Pour it into the main part of the tablet, moving the saucepan as you pour so as to get a thin layer all over.

5 Cut a pencil length of dowel and sandpaper the cut ends smooth. Sharpen one end in the pencil-sharpener.

A scroll

You will need

- 2 pieces of 5 mm dowel, each 30 cm long
- 4 large wooden beads with a 5 mm hole
- pencil
- PVA glue
- sheet of papyrus or strong paper
- ruler
- scissors
- masking tape

What to do

1 Fit the beads on the ends of the dowel. Use a pencil to mark how far along each piece of dowel is covered by the beads.

2 Remove the beads. Spread the part of the dowel where they fit with glue. Now put the beads in place and leave the glue to set.

3 Measure the height of papyrus that will fit on the dowel rollers between the beads. Mark a long strip this high on the papyrus and cut it out.

4 Tape one end of the papyrus to one roller. Then spread glue on the 4 cm of papyrus close to the roller, and wind the papyrus tightly round the roller to hide the tape. Do the same with the other roller.

4 Precious writings

The long history of the Jewish people was told in their special writings, the Hebrew scriptures. Every week, the Jewish people gathered at their local meeting place, the synagogue, to hear the scriptures read aloud.

Jesus reads from a scroll

The precious Hebrew scriptures were written on scrolls. These were kept safe in a box in the synagogue.

One sabbath, when Jesus was a grown man, he took his turn to read at the synagogue.

He unrolled the scroll and found a passage in the book of the prophet Isaiah. It spoke of God's ancient promise to send the nation a special king—one who would set them free to live as God's people should.

Then he rolled up the scroll, gave it back to the attendant and sat down.

Everyone was looking at him. In the last little while Jesus had become a travelling preacher. What was he going to say to them?

Jesus spoke: 'This passage of scripture has come true today, as you heard it being read.' He began to explain more about God, telling them what it meant to live as God's people.

'Would you believe it,' they whispered. 'He's just the son of Joseph the carpenter. How dare he speak like this, like he was some prophet?'

'Think about some of the stories of our people,' Jesus continued. Think of some of the great prophets who told people about God. Their own people threw them out… yet they worked wonders amongst foreigners. A prophet is never welcomed in his own town.'

Suddenly, the people were angry. They formed a mob around Jesus and hustled him out of the building. They jostled him towards a craggy precipice, hoping to hurl him over the edge and stone him to death.

At the last moment, Jesus simply walked away.

The Spirit of the Lord
is upon me,
because he has chosen
me to bring good news
to the poor.
He has sent me to
proclaim liberty to the
captives
and recovery of sight to
the blind;
to set free the oppressed
and announce that the
time has come
when the Lord will save
his people.

5 Remembering God's laws

The Jewish people believed that God had given them laws: laws that would guide them in leading lives that were good and gentle, fair and honest. The law was very important indeed. Here is part of it:

> Hear O' Israel, the Lord is our God, the Lord alone. You shall love the Lord your God with all your heart and with all your soul and with all your might. Take to heart these instructions with which I charge you this day. Impress them upon your children. Recite them when you stay at home and when you are away, when you lie down and when you get up. Bind them as a sign on your hand and let them serve as a symbol on your forehead; inscribe them on the doorposts of your house and on your gates.

It became the custom to make small leather containers that could be tied on to the head or the arm. Inside were small pieces of parchment, each with words from the law written in tiny, perfect Hebrew letters.

☯ Leather pockets to be worn bound to the forehead. Inside each is a part of God's laws. Jesus criticized people who chose to wear a pocket larger than standard. He said they were simply showing off how holy they were.

The most important law

One day, a teacher of the law came to Jesus. 'What must I do in order to be close to God forever?' he asked.

'What do our scriptures say?' said Jesus.

The man replied, ' "Love the Lord your God with all your heart, with all your soul, with all your strength, and with all your mind" and "Love your neighbour as you love yourself." '

'Quite right,' said Jesus.

'But who is my neighbour?' asked the man.

Jesus told a story:

'There was once a man who was travelling from Jerusalem to Jericho. On the lonely desert road, robbers attacked him, beat him, took everything he had, and left him for dead.

'Now a priest was going that way. He saw the man, but he walked by on the other side of the road.

'Then one of the temple officials came along. He was concerned at what he saw, and walked over to the man to look more closely. Then he hurried away.

'Next, a Samaritan came along.'

There was an awkward hush. Everyone listening knew that Samaritans and Jews hated one another and wanted nothing to do with each other. Jesus continued his story:

'The Samaritan saw the man, and he wanted to help. So he went over to him, tended his wounds and bandaged them. He put the man on his donkey, and took him to an inn.

' "Take care of this man for me," he asked the innkeeper. "Here is money to pay you for your trouble. If you spend more, I will repay you on my way back." '

Then Jesus asked a question: 'Which of the three acted like a neighbour towards the man attacked by robbers?'

'The one who was kind to him,' replied the man.

Jesus said, 'You go, then, and do the same!'

Religious leaders from the time of Jesus. Above is a rabbi, a teacher, shown wearing a large leather 'pocket' or phylactery on his forehead. On the right is a temple priest, wearing a white tunic with a sash and a turban as the law itself demanded. With him is the high priest, wearing a blue tunic and colourful overgarments.

A box for God's laws

You will need

- *a piece of soft black leather, vinyl or felt, 15 cm x 15 cm*
- *black buttonhole thread*
- *a sharp, thick needle*
- *a skewer and a thick polystyrene block*
- *strong black thread and blue thread*
- *strong paper*
- *pen and ink*

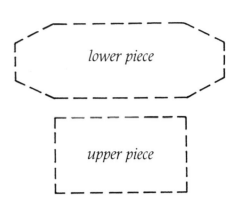

lower piece

upper piece

What to do

1 Cut the piece of leather to the shapes shown in the illustrations above right. (Enlarge the pieces if you want to make a larger box.)

2 Centre the upper piece on the lower piece. Stitch with buttonhole thread using an in-and-out stitch. Leave one short side open.

3 Cut a piece of paper small enough to slip into the pocket you have made. On it, copy words from the Jewish laws. You can use the ones given on page 16 of this book or any others you find in the law books of the Jewish scriptures. The 'Ten Sayings' or 'Ten Commandments' can be found in the Bible, in the book of Exodus chapter 20 verses 1–17. Roll the paper into a tight bundle and tie with strong blue thread. Place carefully inside the pocket.

4 Now stitch the remaining opening shut, and stitch a second time around, placing stitches in the gaps left on the first row.

5 Lay the pocket on the polystyrene and ask a grown-up to punch a hole through with a skewer; then thread three long pieces of the strong black thread through. Line up the ends of each and treat each 'pair' as one. Plait these three pairs into a cord. Knot the end. Repeat for the other side. Use the strip or cord to tie the pocket to your forehead.

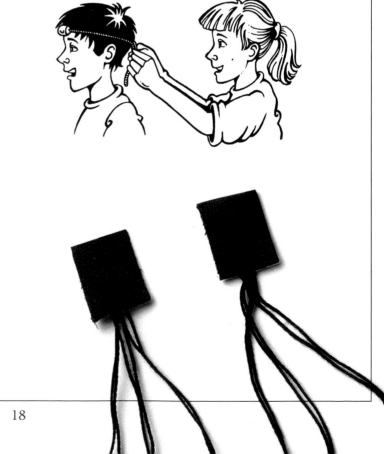

A tasselled shawl

You will need

- *a length of cream or white embroidery linen about 100 cm x 40 cm*

- *scissors*

- *needle and thread*

- *masking tape*

- *blue fabric paint and stencil brush*

- *piece of strong card, about 2 cm x 12 cm. Draw a midway line on both sides and notch as shown in the photograph at the bottom of this page*

- *cream and blue embroidery yarn*

- *bodkin*

What to do

1 Trim the fabric neatly into a rectangle, following a thread in the weave of the cloth as you cut.

2 Turn in about 10 mm as a hem along each long edge. Fold over a second time and tack in place.

3 Mark how long you want the fringe to be, and pull out a thread at this height. Pull out more threads from this top one down. When there are only a few rows of threads holding the weave at the bottom edge, begin taking small bunches of threads and knotting them as shown (see above photograph). Repeat for both ends of the shawl.

4 Now hem both long edges. Use a small in-and-out stitch or a hemming stitch. Remove the tacking.

5 Mark where the three blue stripes will go at each end of the shawl. Stick masking tape on either side and stencil blue stripes on the fabric. (See also the stencilling instructions on page 30.)

6 Make a tassel. Tape one end of each of the cream and blue embroidery yarns onto the notched card and wind the yarn round and round about 20 times. Tape the ends in place.

7 Take a long piece of blue thread and tie it very tightly around the threads about 2 cm from the mid point of the card. Make sure you have a 'short' end that will still wrap round to the mid point on the underside.

8 Thread the long end on to the bodkin and begin making loop stitches around the wound threads. Keep the loops close together and cover the wound threads for about 4 cm.

9 Hold the working end of the blue thread firmly as you cut the bundle of threads at the mid point of the underside of the card. Then curve the bound area over so the start and finish point of your loop stitches meet, and bind in place with several winds of the blue thread. Knot it to the short end.

10 Thread a short piece of blue thread on a large needle and attach the tassel to the shawl by taking a stitch through the open eye of the tassel head. Tie the thread tightly. Make three more tassels and attach them to the other corners.

6 God's laws, God's forgiveness

The Jewish people firmly believed that it was very important to keep God's laws, and Jesus said the same. Jesus also said that God was a God of forgiveness. He was angry with those who smugly thought they were better than anyone elsc in God's eyes. He criticized people who liked to show off just how religious they were and looked down on others.

One of the laws in the scriptures told the Jewish men to make tassels for their cloaks—a tassel at each corner, tied with a blue cord. The tassels were to be a reminder for all time to keep God's good laws. Some people used this rule as a way of showing off. They made extra long tassels for the shawls they wore over their heads when they went to pray, so that everyone would see.

© The long tassels on a prayer shawl were meant to remind the wearer of the importance of keeping God's laws. Men wore a shawl like this over their heads when they went to pray.

The two men and their prayers.

Jesus told this story to people who were sure of their own goodness but who looked down on others:

'Two men went to God's temple to pray. One was very pleased with all the good things he had done. The other was not.

'The one who was pleased with himself stood in a place where he was sure to be noticed. He lifted his long, tasselled shawl over his head, as was the custom, before he began to pray:

'"I thank you, God, that I am not greedy, dishonest, or disloyal to my wife and family... as so many others are. I thank you that I'm not like that man over there. I've kept the laws about fasting, which I do two days a week. I've given a tenth of my money to support good works."'

'The man who was not pleased with himself stood further back, hoping no one would see him. He thought of everything he'd got wrong and he didn't like to begin listing it out.

'"God have pity on me,"' he said. "I've made a mess of everything."

'Now you can be sure,' said Jesus, 'that it was the one who asked for God's forgiveness who got things right. His friendship with God was mended by his prayer.'

The Temple in Jerusalem. Two men are climbing the entrance steps to go to pray.

7_ Storing up treasure

It's so hard being poor. Life is much easier if you have enough money to buy the things you need.

But is it a good idea to make money the most important thing in life? Jesus did not think so.

The rich man

One day, a rich man asked Jesus, 'Please tell me what I must do to be safe with God for ever.'

'You know God's laws,' answered Jesus: 'Keep the promises you have made to your wife; do not murder; do not steal; do not tell lies about others to get them into trouble; show proper love and care for your parents.'

'I have done all that since I was a boy,' replied the man.

'That's good,' replied Jesus. 'Then there is just one more thing you need to do. Sell all you have and give your riches to the poor. You will have riches in heaven. Then come, follow me.'

But the man grew sad. He was very rich.

The man went away, shaking his head. 'That would be too hard for me,' he must have been thinking. 'It's not sensible… not practical…' Jesus watched him go.

Another time, Jesus said to his followers, 'Sell all your belongings, and give your money to the poor. Then you will have purses that never wear out—and riches in heaven. These riches will be safe: no thief can steal them, no moth or decay can destroy them. You have a choice: to value riches here, or riches in heaven.'

ⓒ These money purses can be tied tightly by pulling one of the drawstrings tight and winding the ends round a 'button'.

A rich man loops his money purse on to his belt.

A leather purse and some coins

You will need

- *a piece of soft leather, vinyl or felt*
- *needle and strong buttonhole thread*
- *a skewer and a piece of thick polystyrene*
- *strips of leather or leather thonging*
- *self-hardening clay*
- *rolling pin*
- *screw top from a bottle*
- *scrap plastic container and scissors*
- *acrylic paints and brushes in metallic shades*

What to do

1 Cut a rectangle of leather 10 cm x 30 cm.

2 Cut a triangle from the leftovers and fold into a 'button'. Stitch in place on the main piece.

3 Fold the main rectangle in half. Thread the needle with strong buttonhole thread and stitch up the sides.

4 Fold the sides in as shown in the illustration. Place the folded purse on the polystyrene and ask a grown-up to help you punch a hole through all thicknesses at the point shown.

5 Thread the leather thonging through the holes as shown. Start and end in the centre of the side without the button. Pull the thonging through so the ends are the same length. Tie them together in an overhand knot.

6 Now thread a second piece of thonging through, so the ends start and finish above the button.

7 To make the coins, first cut a tiny piece of plastic to the design you want. Keep it simple!

8 Roll out a small piece of clay and press the plastic on to it. Centre the round bottle top on this and cut out. Remove the plastic design piece, but use the edge of it to mark 'letters' around the edge. Leave the clay to harden.

9 The next day, roll out more clay thinly. Press the dry piece on to the soft clay. It will leave a raised pattern. Centre the bottle top on this to cut a coin. Repeat as often as you like. Leave to dry.

10 Paint the 'coins'. Apply one metallic colour and leave it to dry. Then thin a darker shade to a wash with extra water. Brush it on very lightly.

A fishing net

You will need

- *a large ball of jute*
- *demijohn corks with holes through them*
- *masking tape*
- *large sheet of paper ruled off with lines, each 10 cm apart*
- *metal 'nuts' (for bolts) with a hole at least 10 mm wide*
- *lightweight modelling compound*
- *skewer (or screwdriver)*
- *acrylic paint in stone colours*
- *sponge*

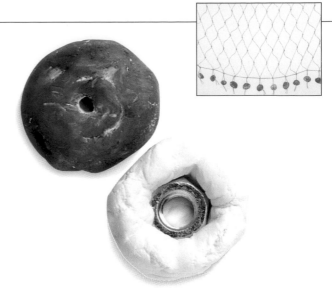

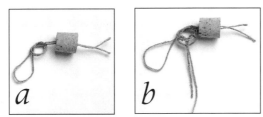

a *b*

1 Cut your long threads: for a net about 1.2 m wide, cut 18 pieces of twine that are 3 m long and fold them in half.

2 Cut a length for the top, about 4 m long, and fold it in half. Knot it near one end (see the knot in photograph a). Loop in a long thread (photograph b). Then thread two corks before making another knot and looping in another long thread… and so on to the end.

3 Lay this top row along a high shelf and tape it in place. Let the long threads hang down. Tape the ruled paper underneath the threads.

4 Begin knotting the long threads in rows. Let one thread from the pair on the left hang straight; knot the other to one from the next pair along. Use an overhand knot. Now knot the other thread from the second pair to one from the next pair… and so on. On the second row, knot the single thread on the left to one from the next pair… and continue knotting in pairs to make a net. Work about 9 rows.

5 Cut a 4 m length of twine for the bottom edge and knot it in as shown in pictures c, d and e.

6 Make 'pebble' weights: take a piece of lightweight modelling compound and shape it around a 'nut'. Use the skewer to push a hole through the modelling material and the hole in the nut, and enlarge the hole so it will be easy to thread on the twine. Leave to dry.

7 Use a sponge to dab colours on the pebbles so they look realistic (the example used dark grey and white). Leave these to dry.

8 Thread a pebble onto each pair of threads, using an overhand knot. Trim the twine so you have just a few centimetres hanging.

c *d* *e*

8_The fishermen and their nets

Jesus lived and worked close to a large inland called Lake Galilee. It was full of fish that were good for eating. So many families along the shore made their living by catching them.

One way of catching fish needed a team of workers in two boats. They sailed—or rowed—a little distance apart, holding between them a long net. Floats along the top edge and weights along the bottom edge held the net upright in the water. As the boats moved along, shoals of fish could be gathered in the net. Then the two boats came close together, and the full nets were hauled aboard.

@ A fishing net with cork floats and stone weights

26

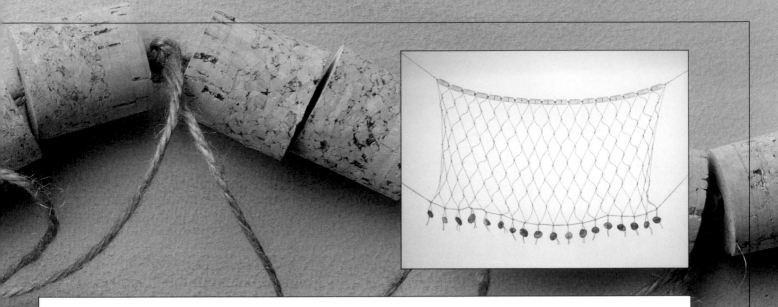

Jesus and the fishermen

One day, Jesus began to speak to people on the shore of Lake Galilee. A crowd gathered, eager to hear what he had to say about God. The crowd grew larger, everyone trying to edge closer to Jesus.

He saw a pair of fishing boats moored nearby. He got into one of them. It belonged to a man named Simon, and he asked Simon to push it a little further out. Then Jesus continued speaking to the people from the boat.

When he had finished what he had to say, he said to Simon, 'Push the boat out further into deeper water, and then you and your partners can let your nets down for a catch.'

'It's not worth the trouble,' said Simon. 'We were fishing all night but caught nothing.' Jesus looked, and smiled.

'If you think it's worth it, we'll give it a try,' said Simon.

When they let their nets down, they caught so many fish the men feared that the nets would break. They waved frantically to their partners in the second boat to come and help them drag the fish aboard.

Then Simon felt afraid of Jesus: this was an amazing catch—a miracle catch.

'Don't be afraid,' said Jesus. 'From now on you will work with me, helping me gather together people.'

Simon's partners in the other boat, James and John, also recognized that Jesus was special. When they heard what Jesus said, they pulled the boats up on the beach, left everything, and followed Jesus.

Two boats trawl a net through the waters of Lake Galilee.

9 Fine clothes

In Jesus' day, most clothing was made at home… and it was a lot of work. Wool had to be sheared from the sheep, cleaned, combed and spun into yarn. Flax had to be reaped and the stalks bundled and left to soak till the stem had rotted away, leaving only the long fibres that could be used to make linen. Then the yarn had to be woven… row after row, hour after hour.

Was it worth hankering after fine clothes?

Don't worry!

Jesus was talking to a crowd.

'Just look at the wild flowers growing,' he said. 'They neither spin nor weave. Yet even Solomon never had clothes as fine as the ones they wear, even though he was the richest king our nation has ever known. Now, if God gives such beautiful petals to the flowers, which last a day, do you not think God will take care of you and your need for something to wear?

'So don't worry about clothes. Make it your aim to live as God's people, and trust God to take care of you and provide you with what you need.'

Men, women and children wore simple tunics with a belt. For extra warmth, people tucked one corner of a rectangular cloak into their belt at the front, wound the cloak to the back and pulled the other end over their shoulder.

☉ Linen tunics with stripes like these were typical clothes at the time of Jesus. (In his day, the stripe was woven into the cloth.) The simple cut of these garments wasted as little as possible of the precious hand-woven fabric.

A tunic

You will need

- 2 m plain weave fabric. Choose a natural colour in linen, wool or cotton
- dressmaker's scissors
- dressmaker's self-erasing marker and a long ruler
- masking tape
- plain scrap paper to protect your working surface
- stencil brush
- acrylic fabric paint
- tracing-paper and pencil
- needle and thread
- sewing-machine (optional)

What to do

1 Cut the fabric into rectangles for the back, front and sleeves (if you wish) as shown.

2 Lay the fabric out flat and use the ruler and marker to outline the stripes. Try to follow a thread in the weave of the fabric. Lay masking tape on either side of each stripe.

3 Lay scrap paper on a large working surface where you can place the fabric flat. Using the stencil brush, dab the fabric paint on the stripe area between the two rows of masking tape. Repeat for all the stripes. Leave to dry.

4 Place the back and front pieces right sides together and stitch the shoulder seams, leaving 20 mm as a seam allowance. Use a back stitch or ask a grown-up to help you machine the seams. Add the sleeves if you are making them, and then sew up the sides.

5 Turn the tunic right side out. Turn 10 mm in as a hem at the armhole or sleeve edges, the neck edges and the hem, and then make a second turn. Stitch in place with a small running stitch.

★ Tunics were worn with a belt. A plain leather belt with a buckle would be suitable. Alternatively, you can improvise a belt by winding a strip of cloth around the waist and tying it with a knot.

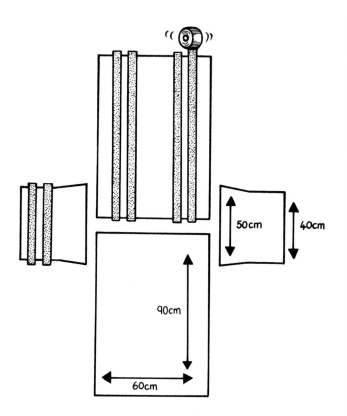

Flat bread

You will need

- 750 g strong flour (plus a little extra for rolling out the dough)
- 1 sachet yeast
- 1 tablespoon salt
- 1 tablespoon olive oil (plus a little extra for cooking with)
- warm water
- wooden spoon
- large bowl
- clean tea towel
- 2 griddles, or heavy iron frying-pans
- pastry brush
- spatula

★ Always ask a grown-up before you start doing any cooking.

What to do

1 Wash your hands. Put the flour, yeast and salt in a large bowl. Add the olive oil and some water and mix with the wooden spoon until it begins to form sticky lumps. Then use your hands to gather all the mixture together, until you have one lump. Add extra water if you need to.

2 Sprinkle some of the extra flour on to a clean work surface. Lift the dough onto it and knead. Use the heel of your hands to push down into the dough, then squeeze back into a lump and push again. Knead for about 10 minutes.

3 Wash and dry the bowl, and put the dough in it. Take the tea towel and wring it out in water. Cover the bowl with this damp cloth and leave the dough in a warm place for about an hour. Let it rise.

4 Squeeze the risen dough down again. Divide into about 8 pieces. Take each one and squeeze it into a flat cake.

5 Leave these cakes in a warm place to rise while you heat the griddles or frying-pans on the stove. Use a medium heat setting.

6 When the surface is hot, rub a little oil all over it with a pastry brush. Put the first two flat breads in the pans, to cook. It will take about 5 minutes to cook on the first side. Use a spatula to turn it over and cook for about the same time on the other side.

10 Flat bread

When you're feeling really hungry, eating a great chunk of bread can take away the emptiness within!

Food for everyone

On one occasion, a huge crowd gathered to listen to Jesus. The day wore on, and the people grew hungry.

Jesus' close companions were getting worried. 'You must send them away to get something to eat,' they warned Jesus. 'We cannot feed them.'

'Have you nothing to give them?' asked Jesus.

'There is a boy here who has a little basket of food,' they replied. 'He has five loaves and two fishes—his own meal.'

'Bring the food here,' said Jesus.

He took the bread. 'Dear Father God in heaven,' he said. 'Thank you for this bread.' Then he broke the loaves and gave pieces to his disciples to share with the crowd. He did the same with the fish.

Somehow, there was enough for everyone. In fact, there was more than enough: at the end of the day, Jesus' friends gathered up twelve baskets of leftovers!

The next day, the crowd came to find Jesus again. Jesus looked at them. 'You have come in the hope that I will give you more food to eat,' he said, sadly. 'But you are not understanding the miracle. Do not spend your life working for food that goes bad. Instead, work for the food that will keep you safe with God for ever.'

'How can we do that?' they asked. 'Give us this bread.'

Jesus said: 'Believe in me, and the things I say. Join in the great adventure that I am leading, and live your lives as God wants. For I am the bread of life.'

The flat bread of Jesus' day might be eaten as part of a portable snack, along with salt fish, olives or other fresh fruit.

Bread was cooked on the hot walls of dome-shaped clay ovens. Inside the oven, the fire had to be kept burning good and hot.

11 Busy cooking

Making a meal from basic ingredients can take hours. In the ordinary home in Jesus' day the women of the household spent a lot of time each day baking and chopping and stirring.

A pot of lentil stew was a typical supper meal. The household would gather around a central pot placed on the floor and a low table, and help themselves by dipping in chunks of bread and scooping up the mixture of vegetables and thick sauce.

Too busy to stop

Martha often felt tired. She lived in a little house with her sister Mary and her brother Lazarus, but it seemed to her that she did most of the work in the house: tending the vegetable garden, fetching the water, grinding corn, baking bread, gathering firewood, cooking and cleaning, weaving and sewing.

Then, one great day, they heard that their good friend Jesus was coming to visit them. What excitement! Today of all days, doing the chores well seemed worthwhile.

Mary was excited too; but when Jesus came she simply went and sat at his feet, listening to all he had to say. Martha struggled on, red-faced and flustered.

Then she glimpsed her sister: Mary's face was shining with delight, her eyes fixed on Jesus.

He was telling stories. He was laughing. He was talking about God—a God who is loving and fair.

'Fair!' thought Martha. 'I'll tell him what's fair!'

She stormed over.

'I'll tell you a thing or two about love and fairness,' she exploded. 'Don't you care that my sister has left me to do all the work by myself? Tell her to come and help me!'

Jesus looked up, with a kind smile. 'Martha, Martha,' he said. 'You worry about so many things. But only one thing is really important. Mary has seen that, and she has chosen to put it first in her life. Nothing is going to change that.'

A low stove had space for a wood fire underneath and two 'holes' for burners, where the pots were placed.

© A stew made with vegetables
from the family garden.

Lentil stew

You will need

- 1 onion
- 2-3 cloves of garlic
- 2 leeks
- a few pods of peas and broad beans
- 1 tablespoon cumin seeds
- 1 tablespoon coriander seeds
- 3 tablespoons olive oil
- 200 g small green lentils
- salt
- water
- parsley

To make the topping

- 1 small cucumber
- salt
- 1 small carton Greek yoghurt
- large bunch of mint
- chopping board
- sharp knife
- pestle and mortar
- large casserole
- wooden spoon
- bowl
- grater
- spoon

What to do

1 Wash your hands. Peel and finely chop the onion and garlic, and throw away the tough base of each. Wash the leeks and cut away the tough green tops and the root. Thinly slice the white part. Pod the peas and beans.

2 Lightly crush the cumin and coriander, using a pestle and mortar. Heat the oil in the casserole and add the crushed spices. Stir with a wooden spoon for about 1 minute.

3 Add the chopped onion, leeks and garlic and stir in for 5 minutes.

4 Add the lentils and stir to mix. Then add the salt and water and leave the pot over a gentle heat to simmer for about 30 minutes. Check from time to time, and add extra water if needed.

5 Add the peas and beans and stir in. Cook for another 10 minutes.

6 Prepare the yoghurt topping. Grate the cucumber into a bowl and add the yoghurt. Chop the mint leaves very small and add these too. Season with salt.

7 Before you serve the stew, check the taste. Add more salt if it is a bit dull. Then chop the parsley and sprinkle it over the top.

★ Eat the stew by tearing off chunks of bread and dipping it in the stew. Then spoon a little topping on to it and eat.

Rich foods

You will need

- *a handful of mint leaves*
- *100 ml olive oil*
- *200 ml wine*
- *salt and pepper*
- *500 g lamb, cubed*
- *1 onion*
- *chopping board*
- *sharp knife*
- *bowl*
- *skewers*
- *grill pan*
- *oven gloves*

What to do

1 Wash your hands. Chop the mint leaves very small and put them in a bowl. Add the oil and wine and a large sprinkling of salt and pepper. Add the cubes of meat and leave to soak for several hours in a cool place.

2 Then peel an onion. Cut it into quarters and cut off the root so the fleshy leaves fall apart.

3 Thread the cubes of meat and onion on skewers in turn. Wash your hands again.

4 Heat a grill and lay the skewers in a pan to grill them. Drizzle a little of the oil and wine mix over the skewers before you put them under the heat for about 3 minutes. Remove from the heat and, wearing oven gloves, carefully turn the skewers. Grill for another 3–5 minutes. They are done when the pinkiness has gone from the meat. Ask a grown-up to help you decide when they are properly cooked.

★*Mint, cucumber and yoghurt topping (see page 36) is delicious on the meat.*

12 _A great feast_

A feast means rich foods in abundance and fine drinks. The table is spread lavishly, and comfortable places are prepared for the guests.

◎ Meat was a luxury in Jesus' day, and it was only served on special occasions. A feast would include a wide variety of dishes and side dishes.

Party giving

One day, Jesus was invited to a special meal. His host was rich and important, and so were many of the guests. Jesus told them a story:

'There was once a man who was giving a great feast. He invited many people.

'His servants delivered the message.

'The important people he invited all agreed to come: "We'll be honoured to attend," they said.

'So, preparations were made. Food and drink were ordered, enough for everyone to feast in abundance. The man sent his servants out with a second message: "Come, everything is ready."

'One by one, they all began to make excuses:

' "I've just bought a field. I must go and look at it. Please tell your master how sorry I am."

' "I've bought some new oxen. I must go and try them out."

' "I've just got married. I'm sorry, I can't come."

'When the servant told his master, the man was furious. "Go out into the streets and alleys of the town," he said. "Bring back the poor, the crippled, the blind and the lame."

'So he did. But there was room for more guests.

' "Go out into the country roads and lanes," ordered the master. "Find people to come: I want my house to be full. And those people who rejected my invitation won't get a look in!" '

A rich man's feast was served at a low table, around which guests reclined on couches, Roman-style. Meals might last for hours.

13 Children's games

Children had little time for games in Jesus' day. From the time they could toddle, children had to learn the jobs that needed to be done to help provide a living for the family. Boys learned from their fathers: farming, fishing, working at a trade. Girls learned from their mothers: tending crops, weaving and sewing, cooking meals and looking after the household stores of food.

Such few toys as they had were usually made at home from odds and ends.

Most grown-ups thought that children were a bit of a nuisance.

Marbles

Marbles were made from small balls of clay and painted. Two players sit a short way apart. They put a marble between them. They each have the same number of marbles to play with—perhaps five each, plus one more.

They take it in turns to roll the extra marble between them, each time trying to hit the centre marble. When a player does, they capture that marble and the other player has to use one of their store to continue play.

The winner is the one who captures the most marbles by the end of play.

 Board games like this one could be drawn in the sand. Grown-ups might carve the board into a flagstone. This board is made from a lump of clay, grooved like stone.

Jesus and the children

Jesus' followers knew that their master had important things to say.

Learned people came with clever questions.

Rich people came with invitations to dinner.

There were even Romans who recognized that Jesus was special. One asked him to work a miracle and heal someone who was sick.

One day, Jesus' followers saw a group of mothers coming to see Jesus, bringing their children with them. What did they want?

'Let us speak to Jesus,' they begged. 'We'd like him to bless our children—to ask God to do good things for them.'

'Oh no,' replied the disciples. 'Jesus is *far* too busy for that.'

Jesus saw what was going on.

'Let the children come to me, and don't try to stop them,' he said. 'The kingdom of heaven belongs to those who come like little children.'

And he blessed them.

Children playing a board game in the sand.

Spare pieces of wood cut roughly to size make simple skittles.

This ball is a lump of painted clay.

The skittles are stood up in a group. Players take turns to roll the ball at them, to see who can knock the most down.

A board game

You will need

- *self-hardening clay*
- *rolling-pin*
- *old, blunt knife*
- *old pencil*
- *acrylic paints in stone colours and a sponge*
- *pebbles and acrylic paints*

What to do

1 Take a piece of clay and roll it out to about 5 mm thick and about 15 cm x 15 cm. Use the knife to cut off the extra—it doesn't have to be very neat.

2 Use the old knife to mark the surface so it looks a bit like a piece of flagstone.

3 Use the pencil to groove the lines, as shown. Leave to dry.

4 Use paint in dabs and swirls, to make the clay look more like stone.

5 Select pebbles to use as playing pieces. If you wish, paint them to make sets.

How to play

The two players each have five pieces.
Take it in turns to lay a piece on a point on the board. Try to make a row of three with your pieces on any of the lines. When you do so, you can capture any of your opponent's pieces by removing them from the board. When all the pieces have been entered, take it in turns to move your pieces along the lines to an empty point next to where they were. Keep on trying to make lines with your pieces.
The first player to have only two pieces left loses.

A shepherd's sling

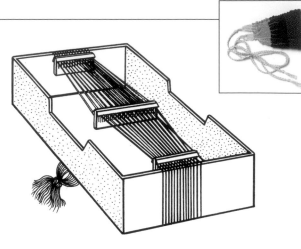

A sling is a real weapon. Ask a grown-up before you try using one, and only load it with soft, light missiles. Never use it where it might hit someone else.

You will need

- *flat sheets of plastic cut from a large ice-cream container, as shown in the photograph below*
- *scissors*
- *thin, strong yarn (such as crochet thread)*
- *cardboard fruit box or similar*
- *masking tape*
- *tapestry wool in several different colours*
- *long weaving needles*

What to do

1 Cut the plastic into the pieces shown below. Snip 2 of them with 14 slits close together, and the third with 27 slits twice as far apart. The result is a bit like combs.

2 Cut 27 pieces of thin yarn, each piece 1.2 m long.

3 Tie the threads round the box, spacing them evenly as shown in the illustration. Knot the ends of the threads on the underside to hold the threads tight and to stop the ends tangling. Insert the combs: first put in the central comb, with a thread in every notch. Then put in the end combs: put the first thread in the first slit, then put a pair of threads in the next thirteen slits. Fasten the top of the slits with masking tape so the threads won't slip out.

4 Begin weaving with thin yarn next to one end comb for about 10 rows. Then tie in one thickness of a chosen colour of tapestry wool and weave a few more rows. Take care to leave the wool loose as you turn each row, so the piece of weaving gets wider as you work closer to the comb in the middle of the loom.

5 After you have woven about 4 cm, knot in a double thickness of the next colour and keep weaving for another 4 cm. For the widest part, knot in a triple thickness of another colour.

6 When you reach the comb in the middle, remove the tape and ease the threads out of the notches. You have reached the widest part. Continue weaving with the triple thickness as before, then with two, then one and finally with the thin yarn to create the narrowing shape as you reach the second end comb.

7 Carefully untie the yarn from the box and smooth it out. Lift the masking tape off the end combs. Taking just nine threads at a time, knot the yarn close to the weaving as shown in the photograph on page 44.

8 Take another knot a little further away using all 27 threads together. Then divide the yarn into three bunches of nine and plait to the end. Knot the end so it does not come undone.

★*You can make a good missile with a lump of ultra-light air-drying modelling compound painted to look like a pebble. DO NOT WEIGHT THE MISSILE.*

14 Shepherds and their sheep

Imagine a scene on the hills round Galilee: the sun is setting, the sky is getting darker. Over the crest of a hill comes a shepherd. He calls to his sheep, a long, straggly flock of jostling animals, following in a line behind him. He leads them to a little stone-walled enclosure: the sheepfold.

The sheep run in the narrow gateway. He settles himself in the door. Now the sheep are safe inside. Who or what would dare break into the fold over the walls, which are topped with sharp, spiny branches? Who would dare attack the shepherd to get at the sheep?

Well, if any danger does come close, the shepherd is ready. He has a strong stick to beat off robbers. Since he was a lad he has known how to throw a stone from his sling, whirling it quickly above his head before launching a stone at any wild animal.

He is ready for anything. He cares for his sheep. They know his voice, and they follow him.

The good shepherd

People wondered what Jesus was trying to do—a wandering preacher with a great crowd of followers. What was he trying to do?

Jesus said, 'I am the gate for my sheep. The people who follow me will be kept safe. In the day, they will be led out to find pasture. I have come to give people life, a life rich in good things.

'I am the good shepherd. I am willing to die for my sheep. If a hired helper sees a wolf coming, he runs for safety… he doesn't care, and the sheep are scattered. But just as God is close to me, and I to God, so my people are close to me and they know me. I will stay by them and die for them if I have to.'

A shepherd lies down in the gateway of a low-walled sheepfold so the sheep cannot escape and no wild beast can enter.

A sling is a simple but powerful weapon. The user places a stone in the flat band, then lets the sling hang by the long handles. Suddenly, with a jerk, the sling is whirled around above the head. Flick! The user lets one of the handles go and the stone flies out. With practice, the aim can be very accurate.

15 Light in the dark

When the world is dark, it is hard to see anything… hard to decide where to go, what to do. Even a tiny flame scatters the gloom.

Sometimes, when a person faces difficult choices, they feel they are in the dark, even though it is bright daytime. Sometimes, when sad things happen, a person feels life is dark, even though the sun rises every day.

What kind of light can chase that dark away?

Tiny clay lamps hold a pool of oil, which burns away slowly as it soaks up into the lighted wick. The simple 'wick-picker' enables the user to adjust the wick by pulling it higher as it is needed.

The light of life

'This Jesus is amazing,' said the people to one another. 'He can work miracles. He can heal the sick. He can make blind people see. He *must* be the one God promised to send us—the one who will show us how to live as God's people—to light our way to God.'

'Ridiculous!' sneered others. 'That's a wrong and wicked thing to say. How can this *carpenter* from some tumbledown town up north be God's Chosen One?'

Jesus said: 'I am the light of the world. Whoever follows me will have the light of life and will never walk in darkness.'

Shine!

'All of God's people must be like a light for the world,' said Jesus. 'Your light must shine before others so that they may see the good things you do, and give glory to God as a result.'

Shining for God

Jesus told this story:

'The kingdom of heaven will be like this. Ten girls took their oil lamps and got ready to greet the bridegroom as he and his procession arrived to meet his bride. Five were wise: they took extra oil. Five were foolish: they had only the oil already in their lamp.

'The bridegroom took a long time to arrive, and the girls fell asleep.

'At midnight a shout rang out: "Here comes the bridegroom! Come and meet him!" The girls awoke and adjusted the wicks on the lamps, so they would burn brightly.

'But, oh dear! The lamps were now almost empty of oil.

'"Please give us some of your spare oil," begged the five who had not brought any extra.

'"No, no," said the others. "We don't have enough to give away. You must go and buy more."

'While they were gone, the bridegroom arrived, and the five girls who were ready and waiting joined him at the feast.

'The other five arrived late. They banged on the door, "Let us in, we are here!"

'"No," replied the bridegroom. "I don't recognize you as part of the wedding party."

'So be ready for the kingdom,' said Jesus.

Girls with brightly burning lamps welcome the bridegroom's procession to the bride's home for a wedding.

A simple lamp

You will need

- *self-hardening clay*
- *rolling-pin*
- *baking parchment to work on*
- *glass bowl, about 8 cm across the top*
- *candlewicking*
- *olive oil*
- *10 mm thin wire*

What to do

1. Take a small lump of clay and knead it till it is soft. Then roll it out on a surface lined with baking parchment until it is about 3 mm thick.

2. Use the upturned glass bowl to cut a circle.

3. Lift the edges of the circle gently and crimp the edge little by little all the way round till it forms a bowl.

4. Pull the sides to meet, so as to create the shape shown, and lightly squeeze to make them just join. Leave to dry.

5. Thread the candlewicking into the lamp through the spout, as shown.

6. Pour the oil into the lamp, down the larger hole.

7. For the wick-picker, bend one end of the wire as shown below. Take a piece of clay and wrap it around the bent part. Roll it into a handle shape.

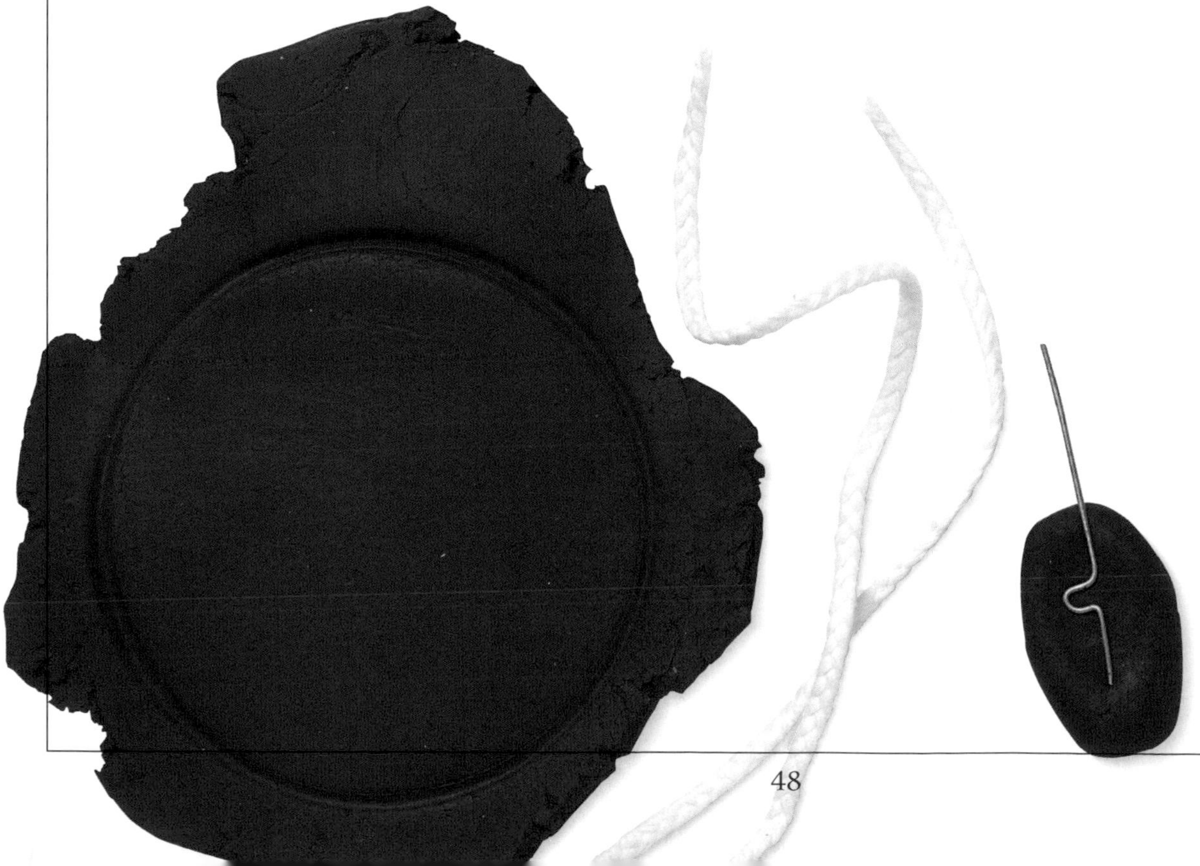

A sower's basket

A fabric strap slung over one shoulder and through the handles of a basket like this means that a person can easily carry a heavy basket of seed.

You will need

- *a large bunch of raffia*
- *scissors*
- *a bodkin*

What to do

1 This basket is made from a very long coil of raffia. Make the coil by bunching together 20 or more strands of raffia. Then take another strand and tie one end round the bunch in a tight knot. Begin making the coil by winding this piece tightly round and round.

2 Every now and then, add a new piece of raffia into the bunch and keep on winding, Keep adding pieces so the bunch stays the same thickness.

3 When the winding piece gets too short, simply pick up a long piece from the bunch and let the short end fall back into the bunch… and carry on winding.

4 A basket like the one shown needs a coil 6–7 metres long.

5 Thread the bodkin with a length of raffia. Tie it tightly on to the starting end of the coil. Then wind the end of the coil into a tight circle and take the bodkin over and under several times to hold the circle tight.

6 Next, continue to stitch the coil to the round in this way: wind once round the top coil only, then stitch once over the coil and through the round below… and so on to make a flat circle.

7 As the raffia in the bodkin gets used up start to include a new piece as you stitch the coils together, and wind it a couple of times round the top coil. Let the last bit of the old piece go free and thread the new piece. Include the old tail end in the next few stitches.

8 Once the circular base is big enough, wind the coil to build up walls and stitch in the same way.

9 Make handles as you coil the last round. Make several strong stitches through the top two rounds at the point where the first handle is to begin. Then wind the raffia over the round below the top coil for a few centimetres. Tie in the top coil so it forms a handle. Take several strong stitches through two rounds to hold the handle down. Make a second handle when you reach the opposite side of the basket.

10 When you are reaching the end, trim the last strands of raffia in the coil and wind on to make a thin tail to the coil. Stitch the thin end down. Stitch in any hanging ends.

MAKE IT!

16 Scattering seeds

Jesus was telling a story about farming.
The scene he described was one that all his
listeners would have known about.

The sower

'One day,' said Jesus, 'a sower went out to
sow corn. As he scattered the seeds in the
field, some fell on the path, and birds flew
down and ate them.

'Some fell on rocky ground. The seeds
soon sprouted because the soil was thin
and crumbly. But when the sun shone
down, the plants shrivelled: their roots
didn't reach down deep enough to
survive.

'Some of the seeds fell among thorn
bushes. The wild plants grew more
strongly than the corn, and it was choked.

'Some of the seeds fell on the good
earth of the field: the corn plants grew tall
and strong. By harvest time they had
produced ears full of grain… some a
hundred, others sixty, others thirty.

'Now you've heard the story,' said
Jesus. 'You think for yourself what it
means.'

The meaning explained

Jesus' disciples did not understand. 'Why
do you talk in stories?' they grumbled.

'The stories are about God's kingdom,'
replied Jesus. 'You are able to understand
what that is, but not everyone can. They
hear the stories, but the real meaning is
lost on them. Now listen:

'Some people hear the message about
God's kingdom but they do not
understand it. They are like the seeds on
the path. The Evil One comes and
snatches away the things they heard.

'The seeds that fell on stony ground are
those who hear the message and quickly
get all excited about it. But the message
hasn't really taken root. When times get
hard, and being part of God's kingdom
brings trouble, they give up.

'The seeds that fell among thorns are
like those who hear the message, but
other things get in the way: the worries of
everyday living, the longing to make a lot
of money, and so they bear no fruit.

'And the seeds that were sown in good
soil are like those who hear the message
and understand it: They bear fruit: some
as much as a hundred, others sixty, others
thirty.'

A sower scattering seeds
over ploughed land.

17 _Unpleasant jobs

There are so many unpleasant jobs that really have to be done. How tiring they are. How dull.

Isn't it great if someone else volunteers to do them for you!

Sandals made of tough leather protected the feet from sharp stones and thorns.

Jesus sets an example

Jesus and his disciples were preparing to share the Passover meal together—the once-a-year festival meal at which the Jewish people celebrated their belief that they were God's special people.

Before eating, the friends all wanted to have their feet washed, following the everyday custom. Washing feet was lowly work. Rich people had slaves to do the job, but they were just themselves—twelve followers of their master, Jesus.

Then Jesus laid aside his outer tunic, tied a towel around his waist, took the pottery bowl and poured water into it. 'I will wash your feet,' he said.

They were all surprised. Jesus was their master, their leader; yet he was not only willing to do the job of a servant: he insisted on doing it right through to the end.

When he had finished he sat down with them. 'You call me your teacher and your master,' he said. 'That's exactly what I am. Yet I have washed your feet. You, then, should wash one another's feet. I have set you an example for you to follow.'

'Listen,' he continued. 'I know that there is trouble ahead for me. I won't be with you much longer… one of you is going to hand me over to my enemies. But before I am taken, I want to give you a new commandment: Love one another. As I have loved you, so you must love one another.'

A slave washes the travel-dusty feet of a guest, using a special pottery bowl.

Sandals

In Jesus' day people wore sandals made of tough leather.

You will need

- *paper*
- *pencil*
- *scissors*
- *cardboard*
- *soft leather, vinyl or thick felt, twice as big as both your feet*
- *PVA glue*
- *leather strips or shoelaces*

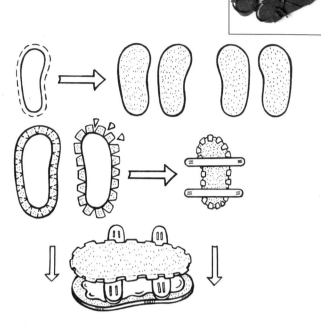

What to do

1 First, stand on a piece of paper. Draw round one of your feet.

2 Then draw around the line again, smoothing it off so it is more like the shape of a shoe sole.

3 Draw another line around this again, about 5 mm away all round. Cut out this pattern piece.

4 Cut out two pieces of cardboard the same as the pattern piece.

5 Turn the pattern piece over and cut two more pieces of cardboard. You will now have two cardboard shapes that 'fit' your right foot, and two for the left.

6 Put the pattern on another piece of paper. Draw a shape about 10 mm bigger all round. Cut out a left and a right piece in leather to this size.

7 Centre the smaller pattern piece on the leather soles and notch the edges as shown in the photograph below. Spread the glue on the wrong side of the notched leather and wrap each of them round a cardboard sole—one for the right and one for the left.

8 Put the smaller sole pattern on yet another piece of paper. Draw round it. Now, on the marked paper, draw strips 2 cm wide across the ball of the foot and at the heel. Extend the strips 3 cm beyond the sole on each side and round off the ends. Cut these two strips in leather for each sandal. Cut a double slit in each end of all four strips.

9 Assemble as shown: first plain cardboard, spread a layer of glue, the two tabs, finally spread glue on the underside of the leather covered card and press that on top as marked in the diagram. Press flat and leave to set.

10 Thread the leather thongs through the loops as shown on the photograph on page 52 and tie at the ankle.

A scourge

You will need

- 6 m leather thonging or string
- scissors
- ruler
- 15 cm hollow bamboo
- masking tape
- PVA glue
- jar
- about 30 roughly-shaped metal beads with a hole big enough to take the thonging
- a piece of leather, vinyl or felt big enough to wrap round the bamboo
- string or rubber bands

What to do

1 Cut the thonging into 75 cm lengths. Gather them together and thread them through the bamboo. Pull the ends through, with 2 cm showing. Fold this back up the bamboo. Tape in place.

2 Arrange the thongs as follows. Stand the bamboo upright in a jar and squeeze PVA glue into the centre of the bamboo, allowing time for the glue to run down so it fills the hollow. Leave the glue a day or two to set. Remove the tape. Trim the bottom ends of the thongs away.

3 Tie a knot in one thong, at least 10 cm away from the top of the handle. Thread a bead. Then tie another knot to hold it in place. Add three or four more beads at intervals in the same way.

4 Repeat for all the thongs.

5 Cut a rectangle of leather big enough to wrap round the handle with an overlap. Spread the underside with PVA glue. Wrap tightly round the handle. Use string or rubber bands to hold the leather tightly wrapped until the glue sets.

★*Whipping bare flesh with a scourge both lashes and gashes the skin. Even this craft version must never be used as a whip.*

★*If you want to make a whip that you can pretend to use as part of a play, use a soft string for the thonging and replace the beads with roughly shaped pieces of a feather-weight modelling compound.*

18 _ A cruel punishment

Many people loved Jesus. He made them feel they were important, worthwhile—welcome to be with him.
Yet some people hated Jesus. Indeed, among his fiercest enemies were the religious leaders of his own people. They were enraged that Jesus was telling people about God and God's forgiveness. They wanted people to listen to their teaching about God. As time passed, they began to plot to get rid of Jesus.

© Roman soldiers used a many-tailed scourge to whip their prisoners. Knotted among the thongs were jagged pieces of metal or rough, hard bone.

Jesus is crucified

It was a dark night in spring. Jesus and his disciples had shared the Passover meal together in Jerusalem. One of the group had slipped away alone—but no one was bothered about that. He would know where to find them, for they were going as usual to a quiet olive grove to rest and to pray.

Out there in the darkness, Jesus told his friends that he felt fearful and sad. They did not understand why, and while he prayed they slowly fell asleep.

Suddenly there was a clanging of swords. Soldiers! Leading them was the man who had slipped away from the group: Judas Iscariot had betrayed Jesus to his enemies, and they had sent men to arrest him.

Jesus' friends ran away. In the long, dark night, Jesus' enemies wove a story of lies. The following morning, they sent Jesus to be tried by Pilate, who ruled the country on behalf of the Romans.

'This man wants to be a king,' they said. 'He is a dangerous rebel who deserves to be put to death.'

'Are you a king?' Pilate asked Jesus.

'My kingdom doesn't belong to this world,' said Jesus. 'If it did, my followers would be fighting for it. But no: it's a different sort of kingdom.'

Pilate decided to have Jesus whipped, as a warning. He let his soldiers mock him, dressing him up as a king, in a purple robe with a crown of twisted thorns. Then he brought Jesus to the crowd: 'It is your Passover,' he said. 'I will set one prisoner free. Shall I let this king of yours go?'

But the crowd was on the side of Jesus' enemies:

'Crucify him!' they shouted.

Pilate gave in; He didn't want a riot. He ordered his soldiers to take Jesus and two other prisoners outside the city walls. There, on a hill, Jesus was crucified.

19 _A funeral_

A funeral is the time when people gather to take a dead body to its final resting place. The person they knew and loved is already gone. Yet they treat the body with tender care as they say their last goodbye.

The tomb where Jesus' body was placed was like a low cave, with a round stone door that could be rolled in place.

© Simple hand-held drums marked the slow pace of a funeral procession.

The death of Jesus

Jesus suffered for three long, terrible hours on the cross. He looked at the people who had arranged for him to be killed, and he said a prayer to God: 'Father, forgive them.'

His friends wept. But one, a wealthy man named Joseph, from the town called Arimathea, knew that he must do something as well as grieve. He went to Pilate.

'May I take the body of Jesus?' he asked boldly. 'I will arrange for the burial.'

The funeral stretcher was brought—two long poles joined with wickerwork, on which the body was laid. Joseph brought costly funeral spices—myrrh and aloes, and these were wrapped close to the body with long strips of linen, according to the custom.

Then, strong men grasped the stretcher handles and lifted it up.

The tiny funeral procession made its way to a tomb Joseph had had cut for himself. The few mourners who dared to show they were friends of a man who had died as a criminal found sackcloth to wear, and streaked it in ash to show their grief. Flutes shrilled a wailing melody. A simple drumbeat marked the steady pace of the stretcher-bearers.

When the procession reached the tomb, the drumbeat fell silent, just as the human heart falls silent at death.

They placed Jesus' body in a low cave of a tomb. Strong men rolled the heavy stone door shut.

But by now the day was at an end: the Sabbath was beginning—the weekly day of rest. Hurriedly, everyone left.

Funeral drums

You will need

- *flexible corrugated cardboard*
- *scissors*
- *two wooden hoops, such as the insides of embroidery frames or hoop-la hoops*
- *masking tape*
- *strips of torn paper*
- *PVA glue thinned with water*
- *brush*
- *tracing-paper*
- *acrylic paints and brushes*

What to do

1 Cut a strip of card 7 cm wide and long enough to fit round the outer rim of the hoops. Tape in place. Cut a narrower band to fit inside the rim and tape that in place.

2 Brush the strips of torn paper with thinned PVA and paste these over the cardboard part inside and out. Make sure the pieces overlap, and use at least two layers. Leave to dry.

3 Cut a circle of tracing-paper 2 cm larger all round than the hoop. Notch the outer edge, brush all over on both sides with thinned PVA. Lay it over the top hoop and smooth down the sides.

4 Add a final strip of pasted paper all round the outside. Leave to dry.

5 Paint the drum white or cream inside and out, avoiding the tracing-paper. Then paint the outside. Cutting a stencil is an easy way to apply a regular pattern. A glue that allows for repositioning is a useful way to hold a stencil in place.

Grape juice

Wine is made from crushed grapes. In the time of Jesus the grapes were piled into a large, round trough and people would trample them. The juice ran out through grooves at the bottom of the trough.

The juice is allowed to ferment—something that turns the sugar in the juice to alcohol. But even fresh juice gives something of the appearance of wine.

You will need

- *red-skinned grapes, washed*
- *pestle and mortar*
- *sieve*
- *metal spoon*
- *large glass bowl*

What to do

1 Wash the grapes.

2 Take a handful of grapes and crush them in the mortar, with the pestle. Tip the mixture into the sieve and hold it over the glass bowl.

3 Squeeze against the mesh with the back of a metal spoon. Tip the crushed remains away.

4 Repeat this process until you have at least a cupful of juice.

★ *The juice from red grapes is surprisingly pale. Red wine gets its colour by letting the juice soak in the skins for a while.*

20 News to shake the world

Jesus' disciples wept. There were just eleven of them now. Judas had betrayed Jesus to his enemies—and now he had hanged himself. The great adventure was in ruins.

They remembered the last supper they had shared: the gentle touch of Jesus' hands as he washed their feet… the command to love one another.

And the meal. He had taken bread and broken it. 'Take and eat,' he had said. 'This is my body.'

They'd hardly listened. Now his body was broken.

Then he'd taken the cup and given thanks to God. He'd given them the cup, saying, 'Drink it, all of you. This is my blood and it proves that God is making a new agreement with people. My blood will be poured out, and as a result all the wrongdoing in the world will have lost its power to keep people apart from God. All people will be able to live as God's people.

'I tell you, I will never again drink wine until the day I drink new wine with you in God's kingdom.'

Then they had gone out. And then… then Jesus had been killed.

His blood had been spilled like any old wine.

Jesus and his friends shared bread and wine at their last supper together.

The empty tomb

A sabbath day had passed since Jesus had been crucified. The next day's dawn was not far off. Some women who had been followers of Jesus went to the tomb, hoping to prepare the body properly for its burial.

In the half-light they could hardly believe their eyes. The tomb was open. The body of Jesus was gone. And then they saw bright shining figures—angels telling them amazing news: 'Jesus is not here. He has risen!'

In the days that followed, more and more people saw Jesus alive again. The terrible wrong done to Jesus had been beaten. Jesus himself came and explained that his new life showed that all the power of wrongdoing was beaten for ever.

Jesus told his friends to take the news to the whole world:

'Go to all peoples everywhere, and make them my followers,' he said.

And so they did. Wherever Jesus' followers met, they told the stories of all he had said and done. They shared bread and wine, as Jesus had done.

And the followers of Jesus still do— two thousand years later. As they do so, they remember their belief that Jesus died and rose again to break the dark power of wrongdoing. They believe that Jesus will come again to take them into God's kingdom, where they will drink the new wine and be safe with God for ever.

Jesus shared bread and wine at the last supper he shared with his friends. Ever since, his followers—Christians—have shared bread and wine to remember his death until he comes again.